William Bolcom

Fantasy-Sonata
and
Dream Music No. 1

for solo piano

ISBN 978-1-4950-8344-0

EDWARD B. MARKS MUSIC COMPANY / EXCLUSIVELY DISTRIBUTED BY HAL•LEONARD®

7777 W. BLUEMOUND RD. P.O. BOX 13819 MILWAUKEE, WI 53213

www.ebmarks.com
www.halleonard.com

Contents

4

Fantasy-Sonata

I shall never forget the first Domaine Musical concert in Paris in the fall of 1959; organized by Pierre Boulez, the new-music group included Paris's most virtuosic musicians (whom I would later join for a summer in Berlin in 1965; see notes for *Dream Music*). I had recently entered the Paris Conservatoire to study with Darius Milhaud, with whom I had already worked at Aspen in 1957 and Mills College in Oakland in 1958–9. I had never heard anything like most of the repertoire on that concert.

Boulez, having had to cover for the ailing Hans Rosbaud for earlier concerts that season, finally was listed as conductor of the ensemble for, I believe, the first time ever. I remember the Schoenberg Kammersymphonie (the one piece I did know) played at what seemed double-speed, but my strongest memory is of a stunning piece for three orchestras, *Allelujah II* by Luciano Berio. The Boulez-Berio-Stockhausen triumvirate was paramount in the European new-music scene. Webern was considered the avatar of a new, serially oriented, often-aggressive music shorn of tonality and free from tradition. I was simply bowled over by this musical world's utter newness (the newest music I had played up to then was of Bartók and Hindemith).

Returning to the States in 1961, I found nothing but rejection of the whole European scene in New York. While earning my doctorate at Stanford, I began to play music of those three composers (and others like Henri Pousseur and Olivier Messiaen, from whom I never took composition lessons, but did attend his course at the Paris Conservatoire in *analyse musicale*) in San Francisco and the Bay Area, about the only place along with Los Angeles showing much interest in this body of work. It would be a fairly long time before New York embraced this music at all, mostly following Boulez's taking the helm of the New York Philharmonic.

My 1961 *Fantasy-Sonata* (there were only small revisions in 1962) is influenced naturally by my new familiarity with these masters and my longtime deep love of Charles Ives, both combined in the sonata. Though there are twelve-tone passages (for example the theme of the Variations), I don't believe there is much trace of the ideological bent of that era to crush any reference to past musical language as so many Europeans sought to do. I had simply never undergone the trauma of World War II which had impelled so many artists to repudiate anything from past music, fearing its possible fault for *les grandes nuits européennes* (cf. Wagner's strident anti-Semitism).

Looking at the music of my *Fantasy-Sonata* from 55 years of distance, I have to admit the sonata really is—of all things—in G major!

Glossary:

(1) ⌐▽⌐ or ▽ means: subtract from the value of the note the sign pertains to, according to taste (generally about 1/6 less). [▽ : subtract from whole group.] ⌐⌃⌐ or ⌃ ; subtract much more from note-value.

(2) ⌐☉⌐ or ☉ means: *add* to the value of the note the sign pertains to, generally about 1/6 more. ⌐⌢⌐ or ⌢ ; add much more to note-value. ⌐⊡⌐ or ⊡ ; add an amount between ☉ and ⌢ .

(3) For grace-notes: ♪ very short; ♪ normal; ♪ longer than normal. Care must be taken to distinguish 𝄢 from 𝄢 or 𝄢 groups.

(4) ⌐ 6:4♪ ⌐ = ⌐ 6:♩ ⌐ = for 4 eighths, or 6 for 1 half-note.

(5) S.P. = suspension pedal; cut-off = ⊕ /(Pedal:℘ₑ𝒹 ; cut-off =✳)

(6) **accel.:** → → →; **molto accel.:** → → → →; **poco accel.:** → →; **ritard.:** ← ← ←; **molto ritard.:** ← ← ← ←; **poco ritard.:** ← ←.

Arrows always cover exact area to be affected by either marking.

6

to the memory of William Blake

Fantasy-Sonata

William Bolcom
(1961-62)

I. Maestoso, ma non largo (♪ = ca. 110); *molto rubato*

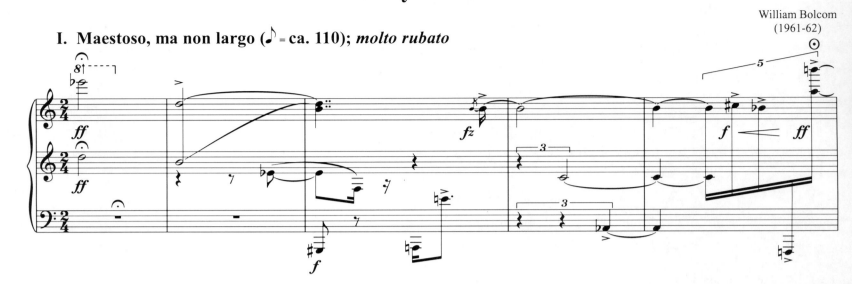

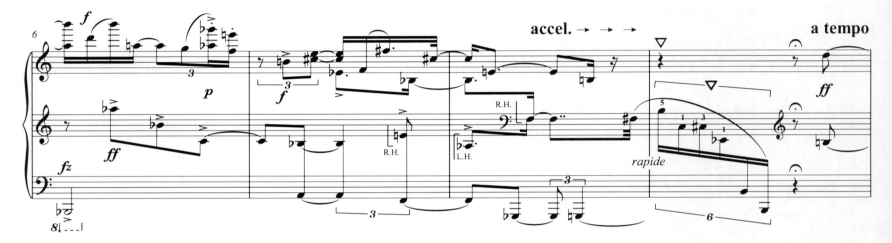

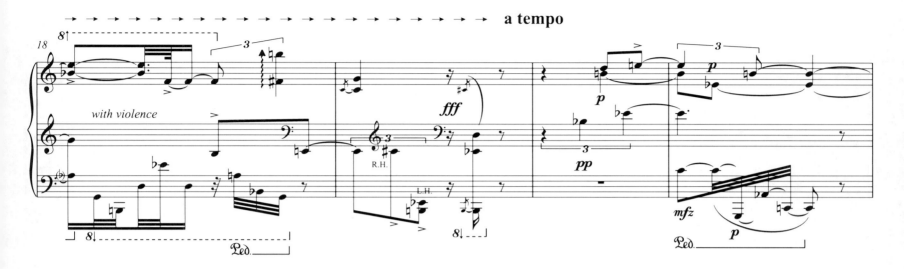

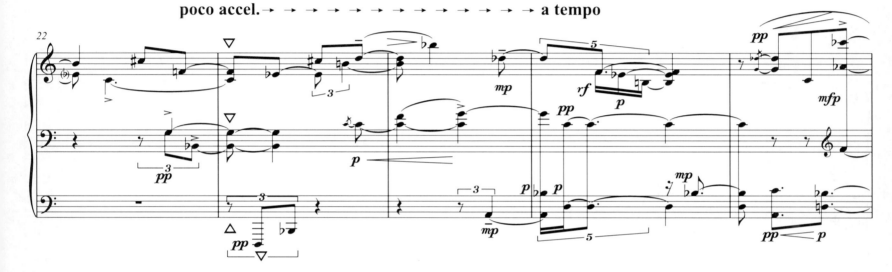

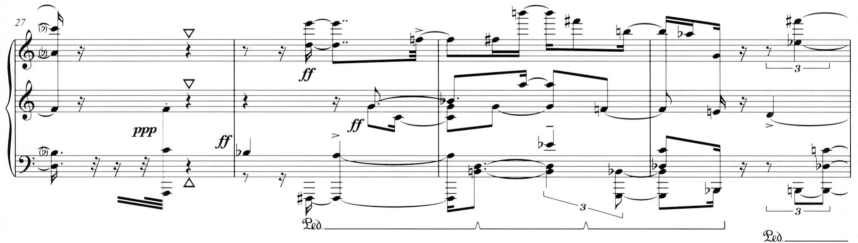

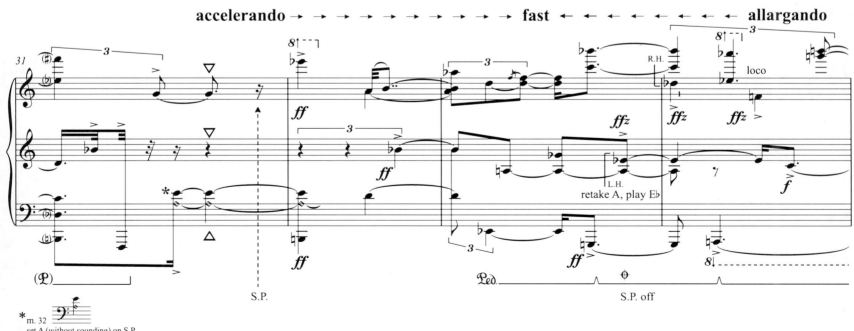

*m. 32
set A (without sounding) on S.P.

8

Note: "retake": retake notes after leaving them, silently.

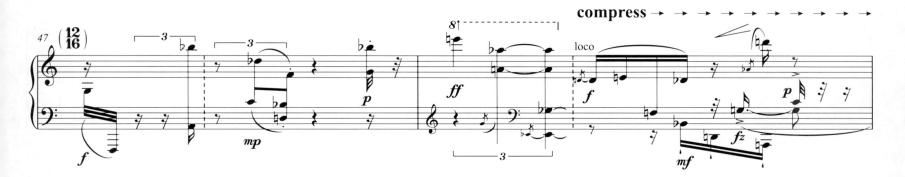

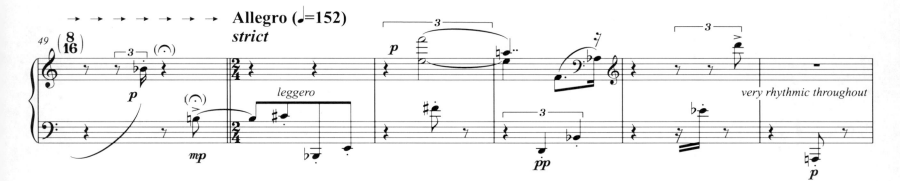

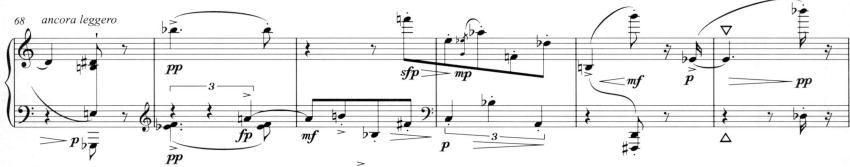

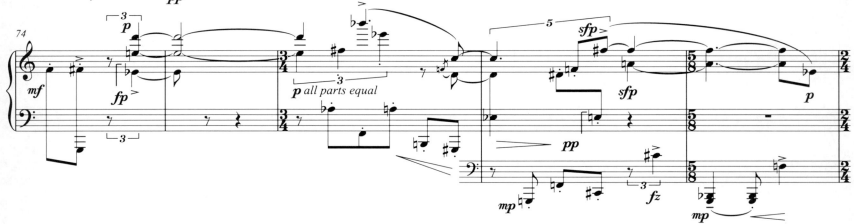

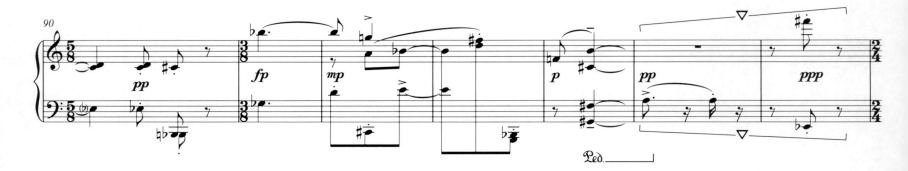

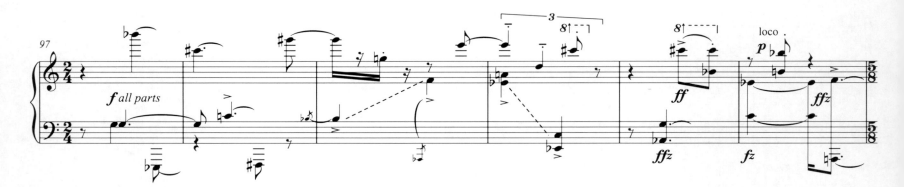

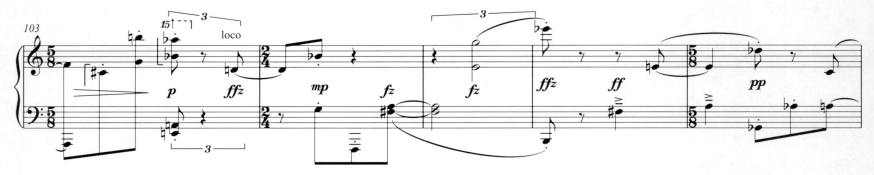

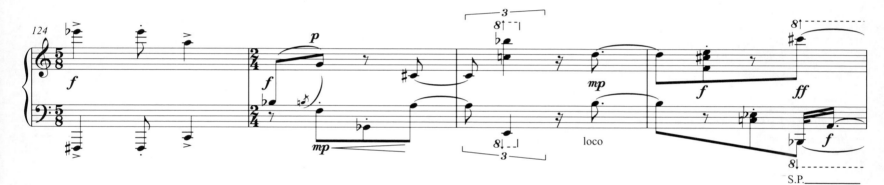

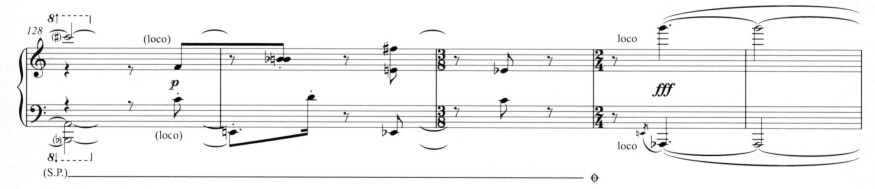

break tension

più mosso (♩ = 170)

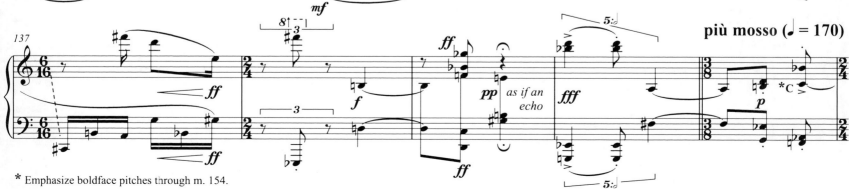

* Emphasize boldface pitches through m. 154.

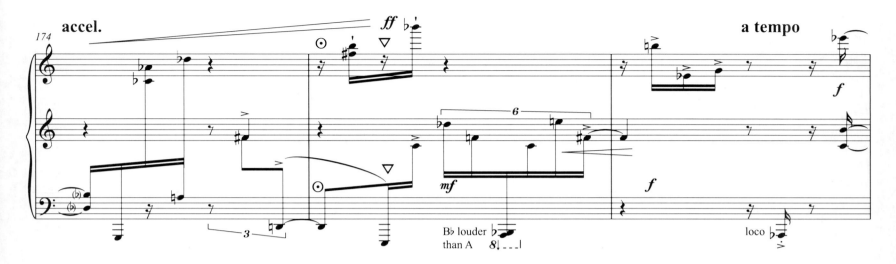

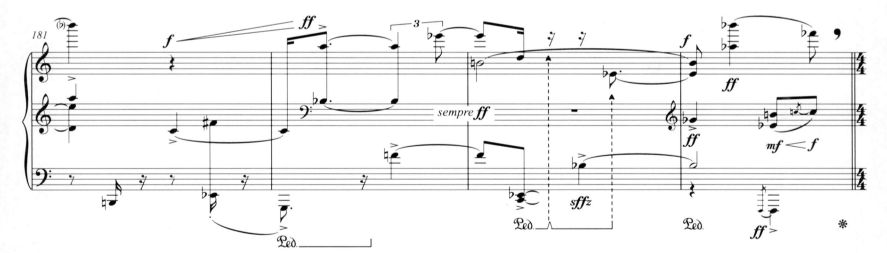

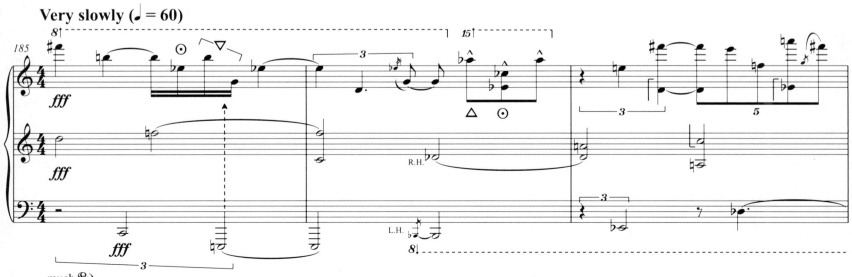

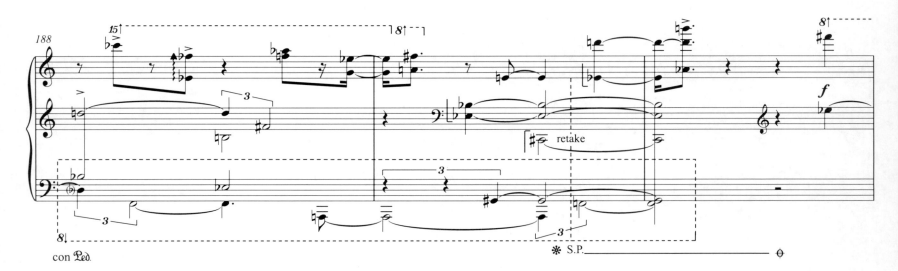

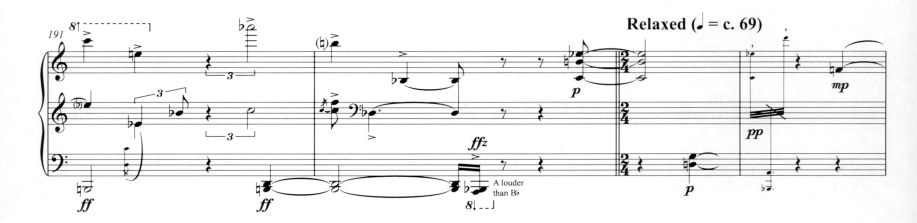

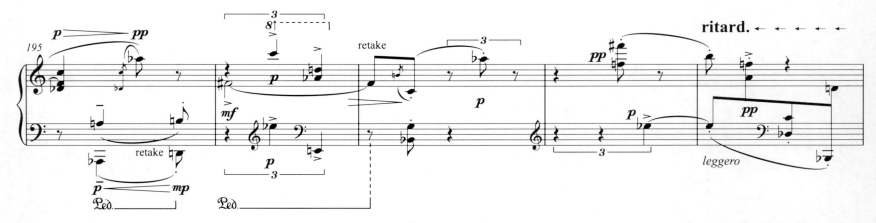

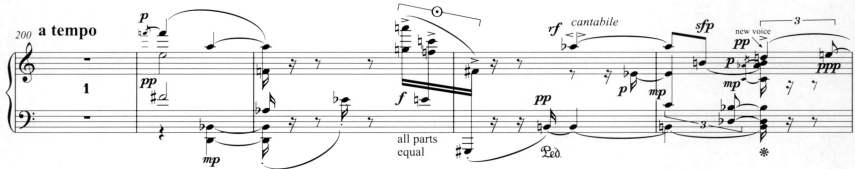

morendo

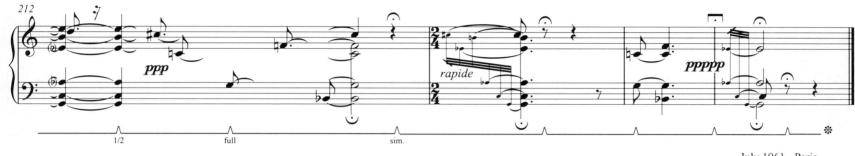

July 1961 - Paris
New York
Stanford

II. Burlesque
Allegro, very rhythmic (♪ = c. 200)

Piano

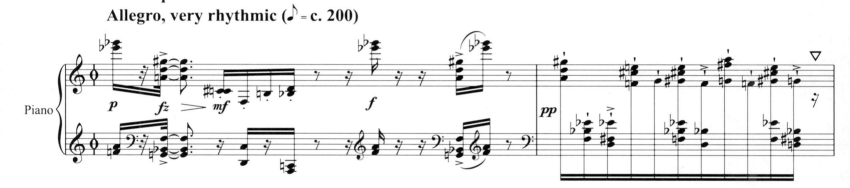

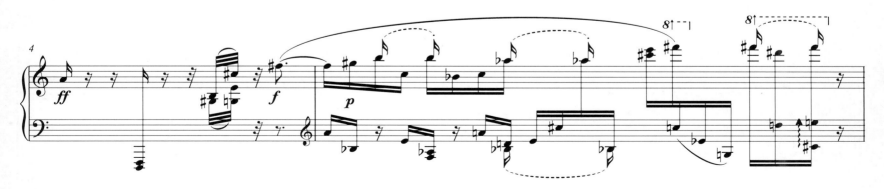

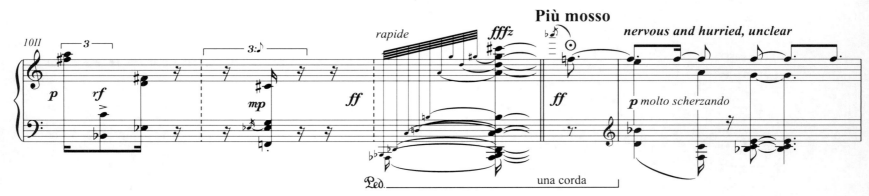

as at first (a tempo)

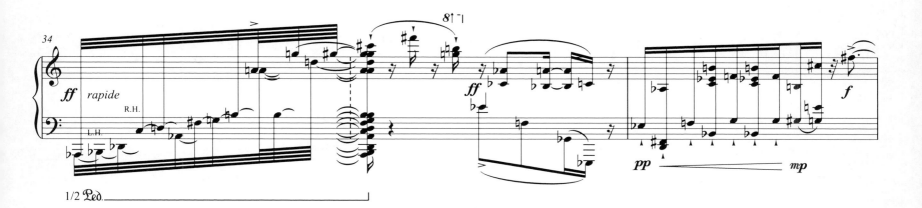

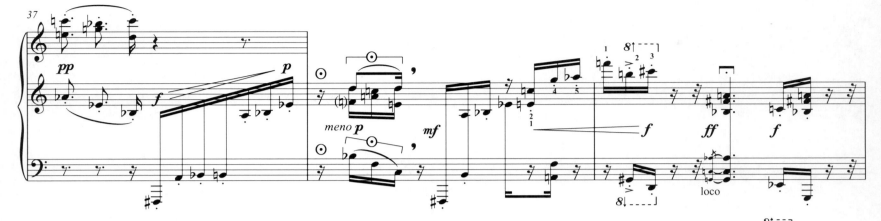

Coda

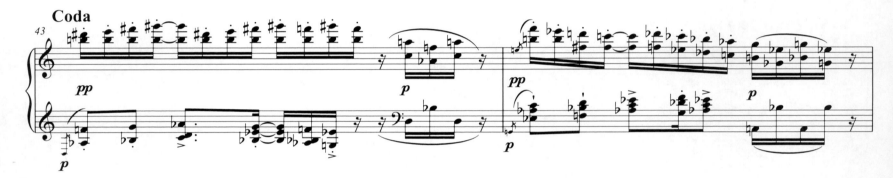

morendo, non rit.

August 1961
Everett, WA

Ped.

IIIa. Andante, cantando ed un poco misterioso
♪ = 60 - 80

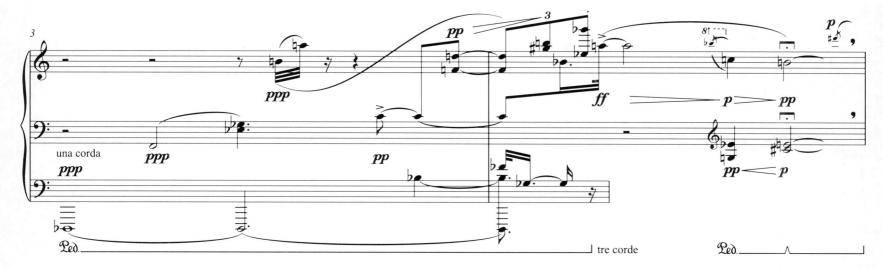

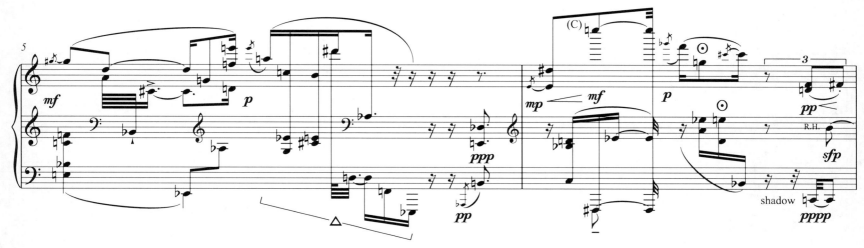

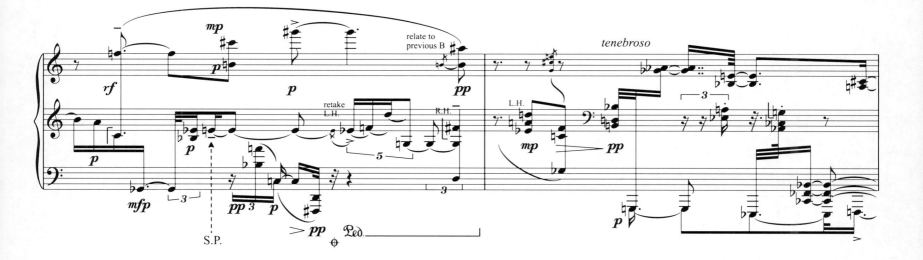

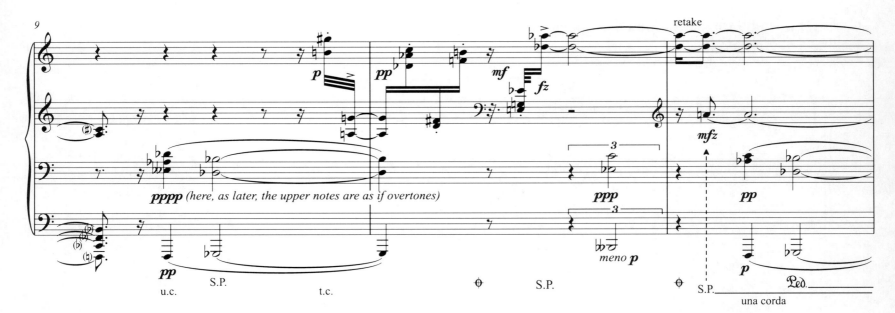

tempo a piacere

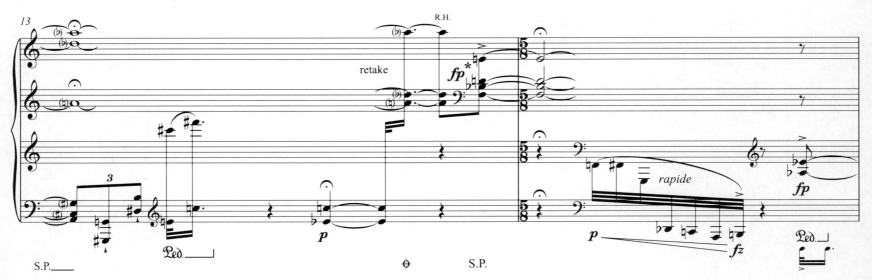

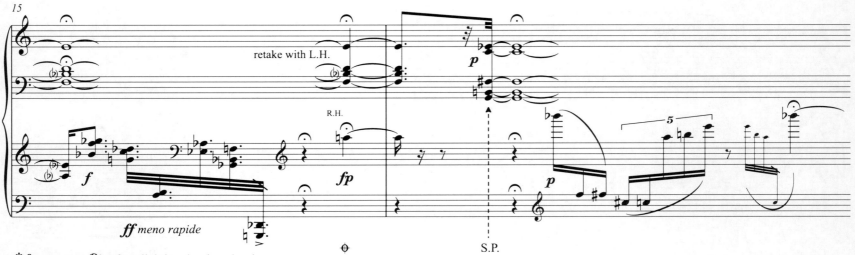

*fp = engage Ped. after slightly releasing chord.

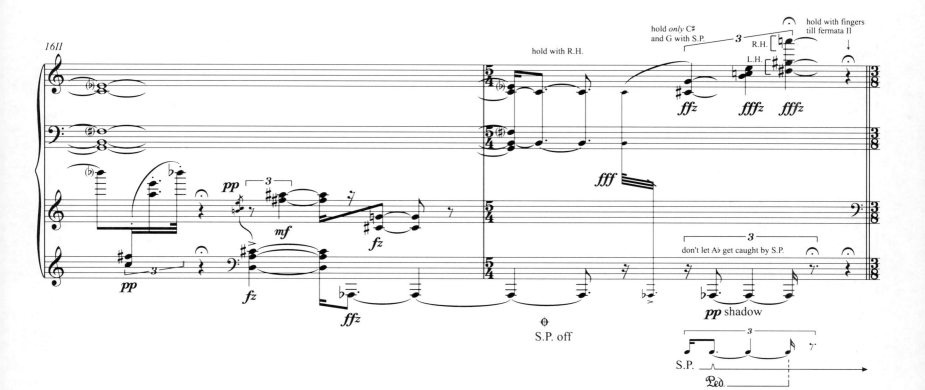

IIIb. Variations (♩. = 88)

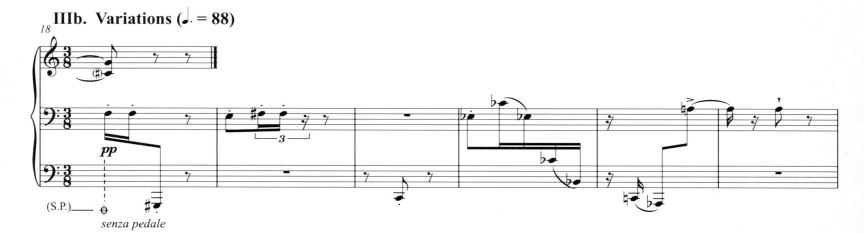

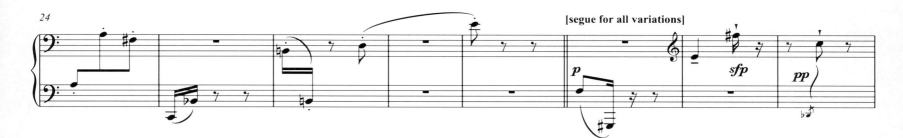

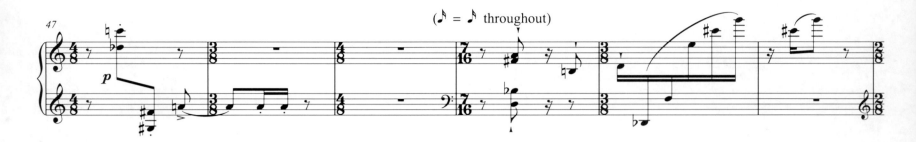

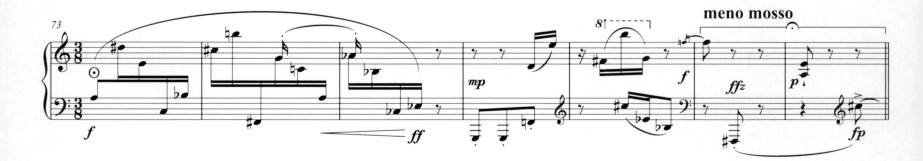

attacca.

IIIc. Andante, come prima, ma ben più mosso (♩ = circa 40)

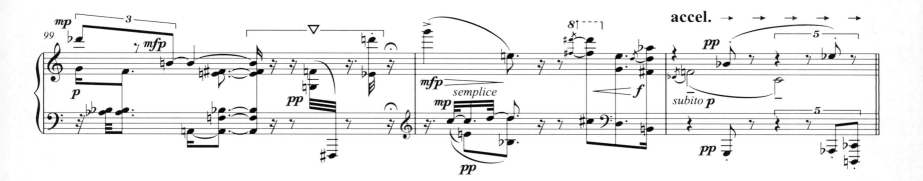

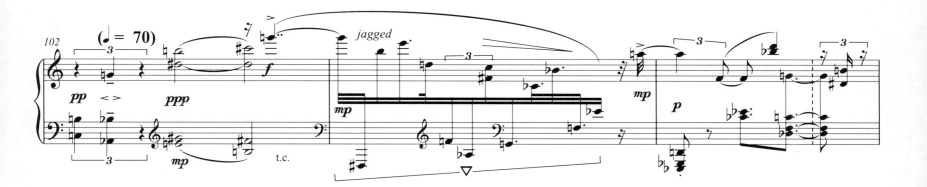

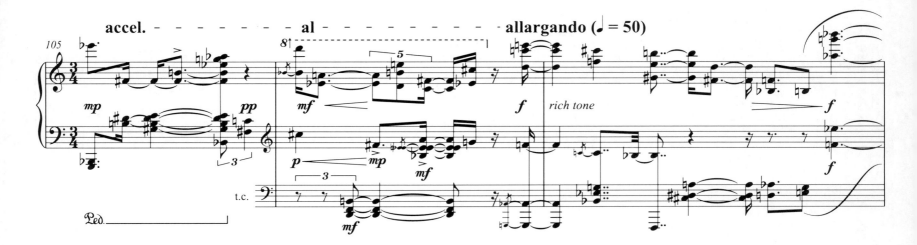

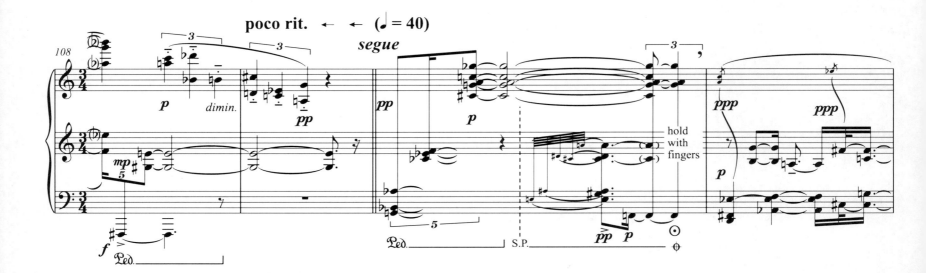

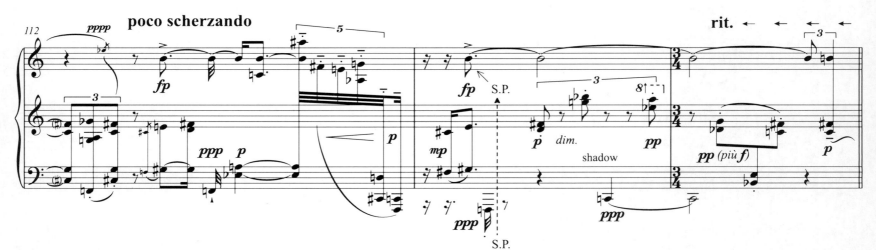

* Third stave from top in brace: as in mm. 9-11, make seem as if overtones to bass notes, even though bass notes come after.

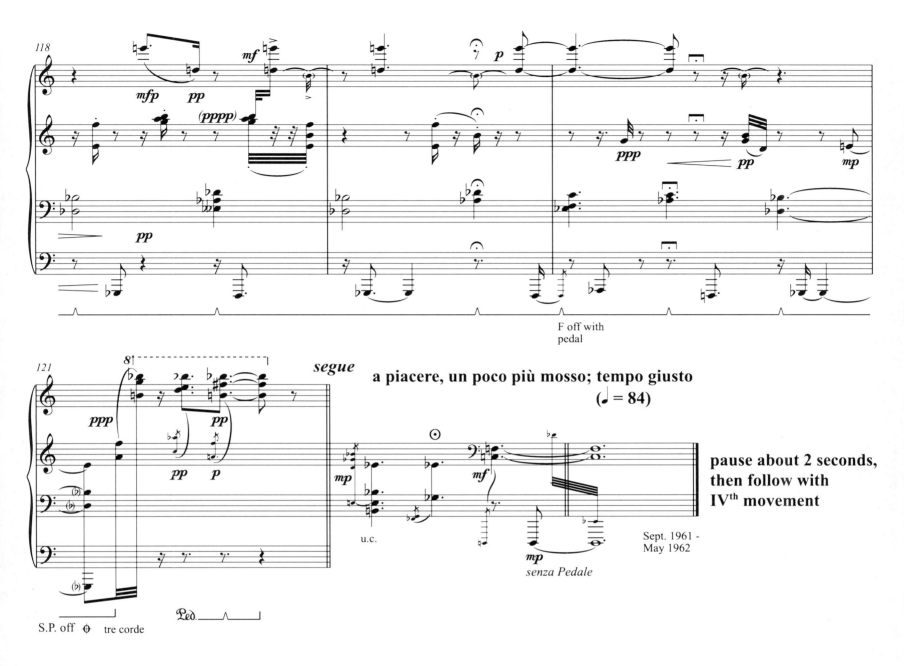

segue

a piacere, un poco più mosso; tempo giusto
(♩ = 84)

pause about 2 seconds,
then follow with
IVth movement

Sept. 1961 -
May 1962

IV. Finale: Burlesqued Variations and Coda (♩. = c. 88)

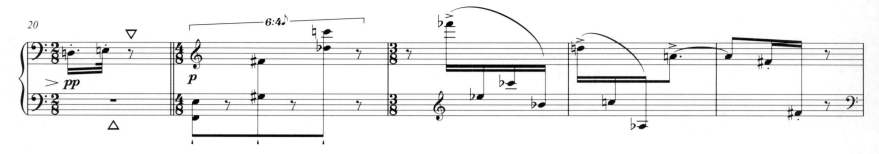

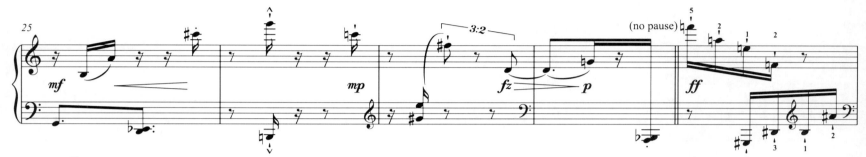

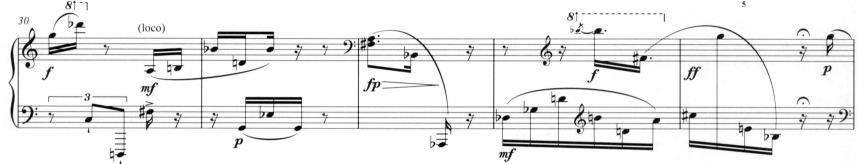

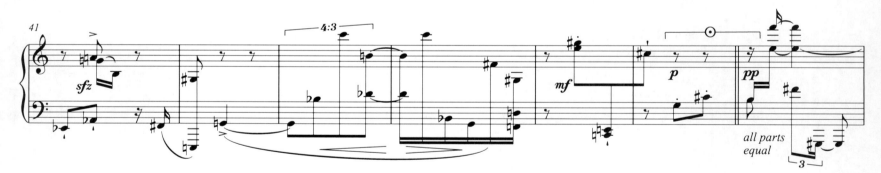

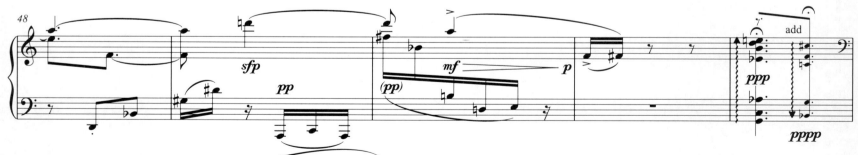

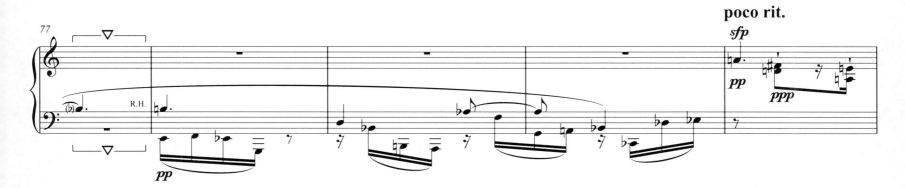

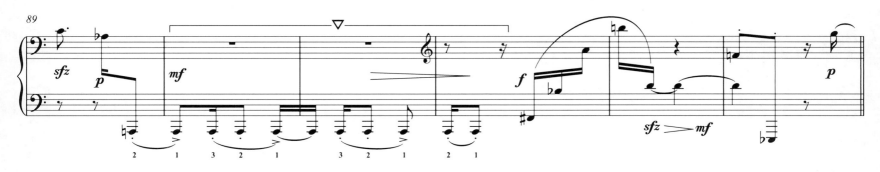

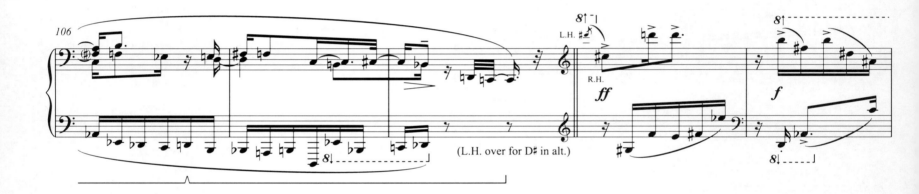

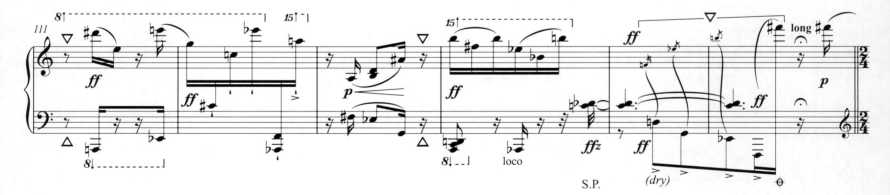

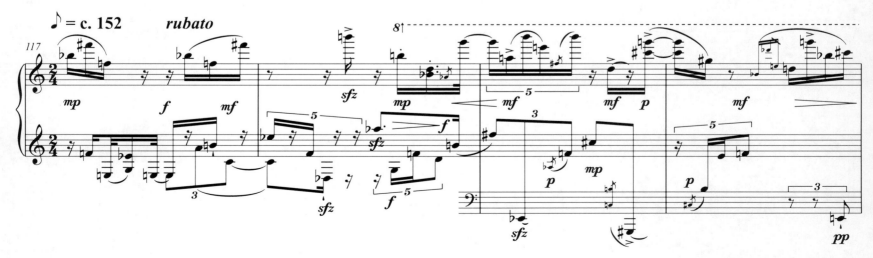

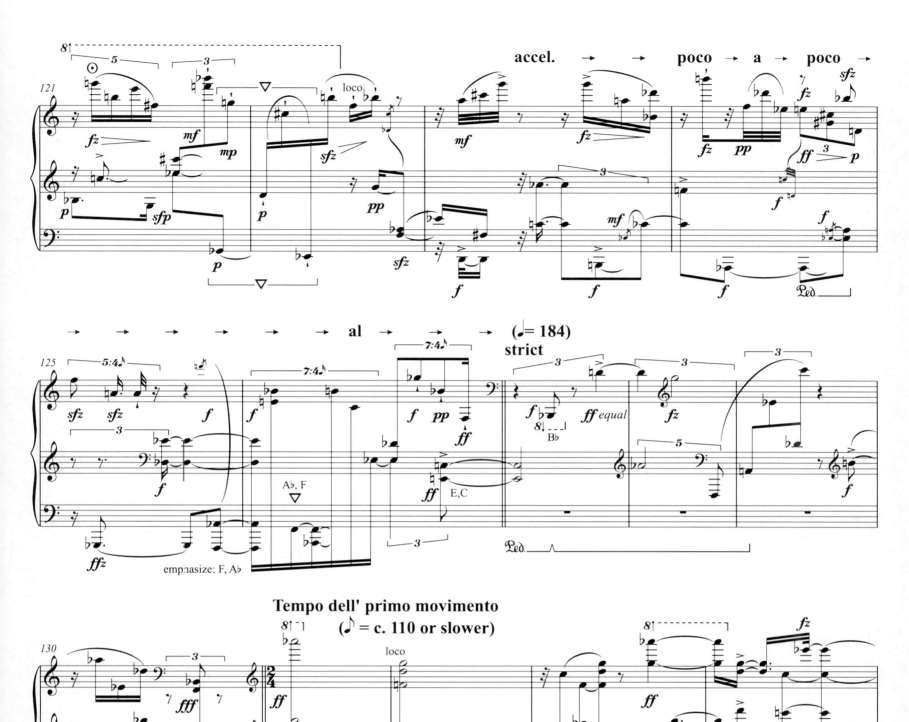

accel. → → poco → a → poco →

→ → → → → → al → → → (♩ = 184)
strict

Tempo dell' primo movimento
(♪ = c. 110 or slower)

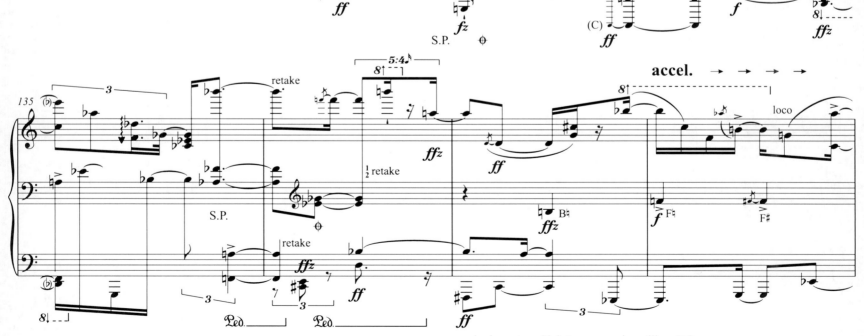

emphasize notes with letter names given till m. 148

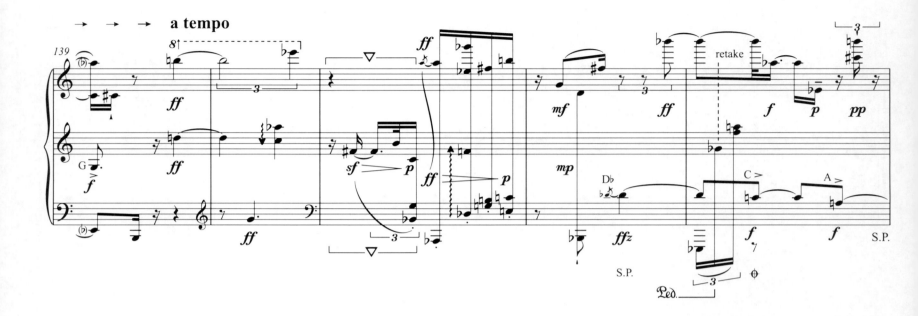

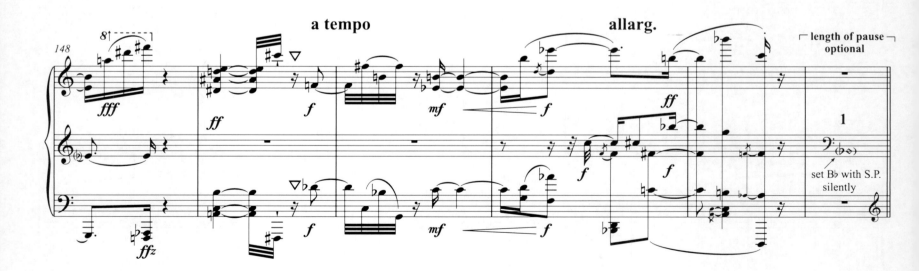

Coda
(1 tactus = 69 m.m.)*

*   The tactus markings in the third staff down show where the "beat" comes in relation to all elements above and below it. More care should be taken to relate all elements to each other, than a strict following of placement between tactuses. The last mark on each line equals the first of the next.

** The tactuses come approximately at the space between two 69 m.m. beats.

*** Here, since pedal is down the ♪ ♪ ♪ grace note differences are a matter of touch.

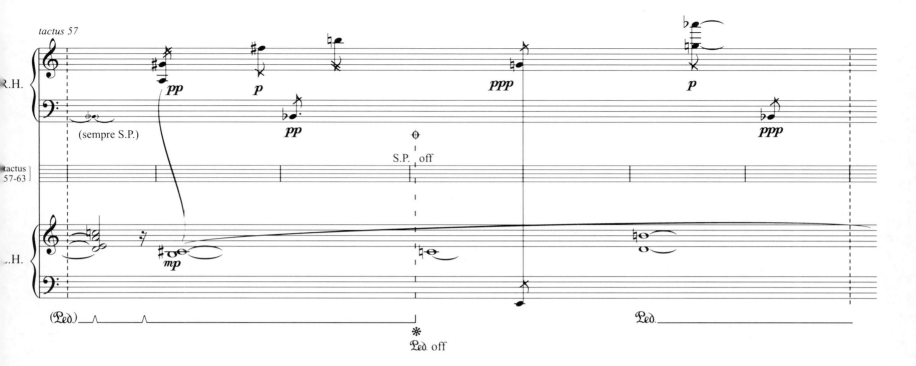

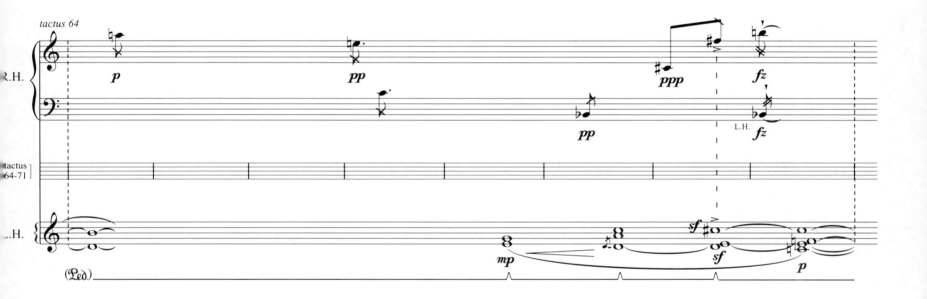

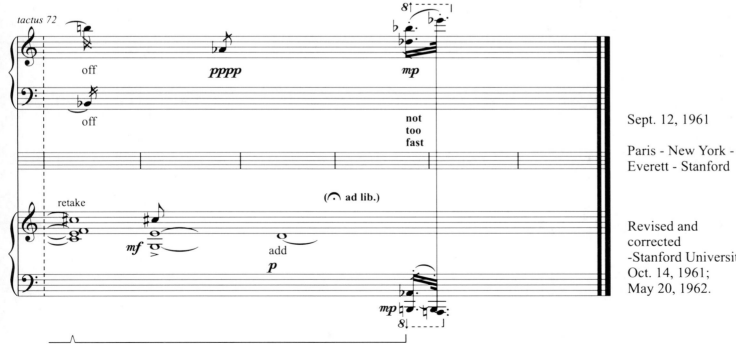

Sept. 12, 1961

Paris - New York -
Everett - Stanford

Revised and
corrected
-Stanford University,
Oct. 14, 1961;
May 20, 1962.

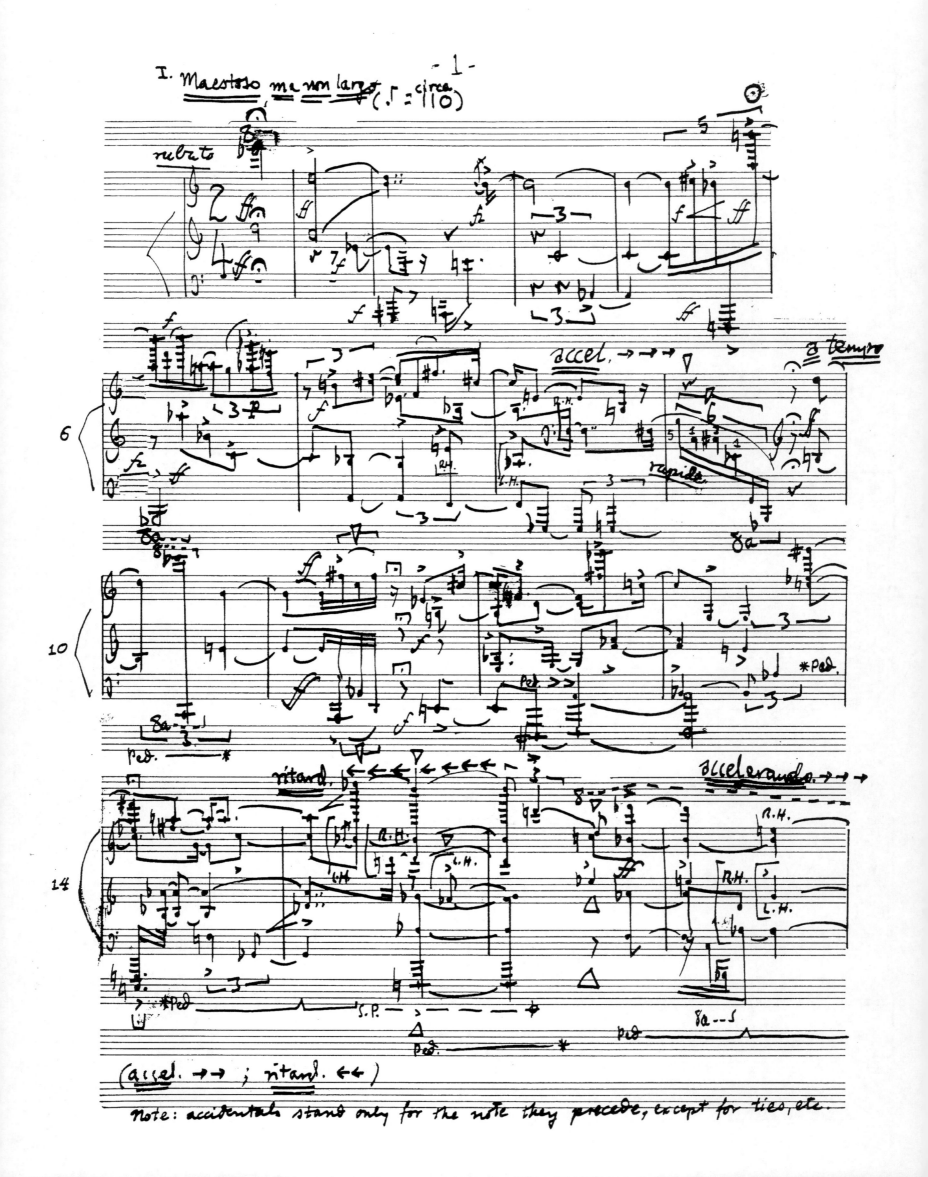

Dream Music No. 1

Dream Music, from 1965, turned out to be the first of three pieces derived from music I viewed as a score for or heard in dreams. For me, dreaming music is a very occasional occurrence and doesn't happen for years on end, the most recent time being what became a short passage in my 2008 band symphony. There are three Dream Musics: No. 2 for percussion ensemble and No. 3 for small chamber group.

Dream Music was premiered in Berlin while I was one of two pianists (the other was Frederic Rzweski) as guest members of Pierre Boulez's Domaine Musical—a Paris virtuoso performance group dedicated to new music—during the summer of 1965 in Berlin, and residing at the Westdeutscher Rundfunk (radio-broadcast) building. Boulez had entrusted the running of Domaine Musical to Luciano Berio, and we played a wide range of composers; I remember music by Gilbert Amy, Iannis Xenakis, and Vinko Globokar, a brilliant trombonist-composer, among many others.

Glossary:

1) in sections marked "free," a "white note" means a long note, a black note a shorter one. Any denomination of *large* notes beside these is purely relative.

2) ❯ = normal breath; ❯ = a shorter one.

3) u.c. = una corda; t.c. = tre corde

4) → → → = **accel.**; ← ← ← = **rit.**

5) in free sections: the grace note shows where to end the note.

6) Accidentals affect only the note in front of which they stand except:

   a) in ties:

   b) in beamed note-groups: but

to Luciano Berio

Dream Music No. 1

William Bolcom
(1965)

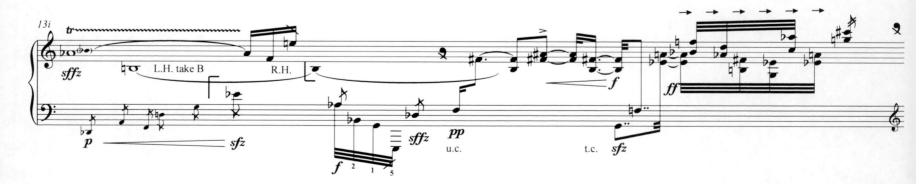

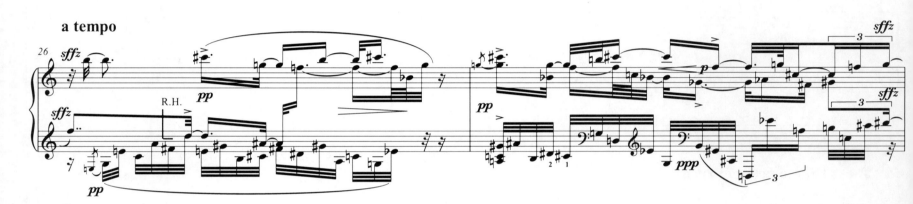

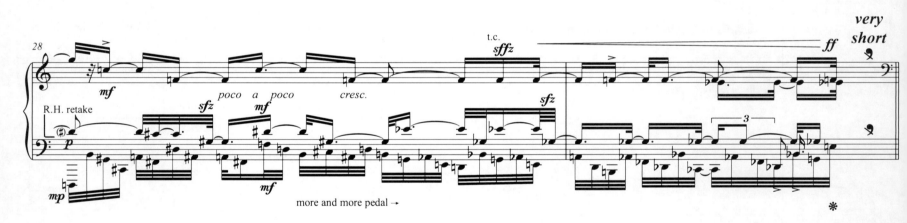

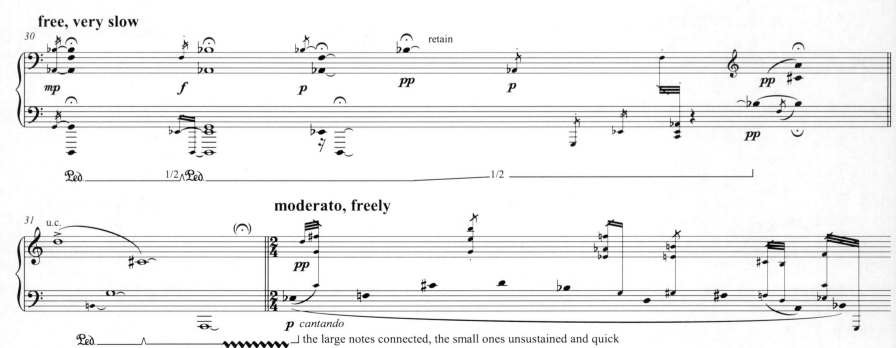

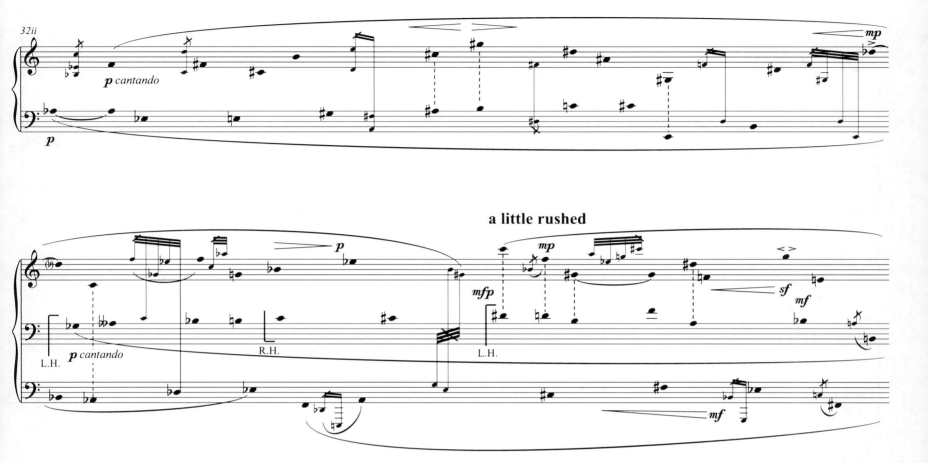

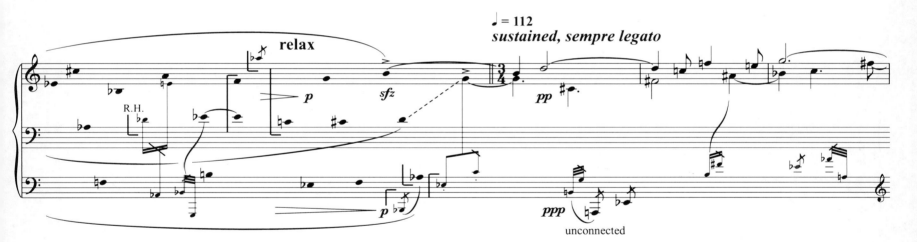

grace-note groups must not be sustained

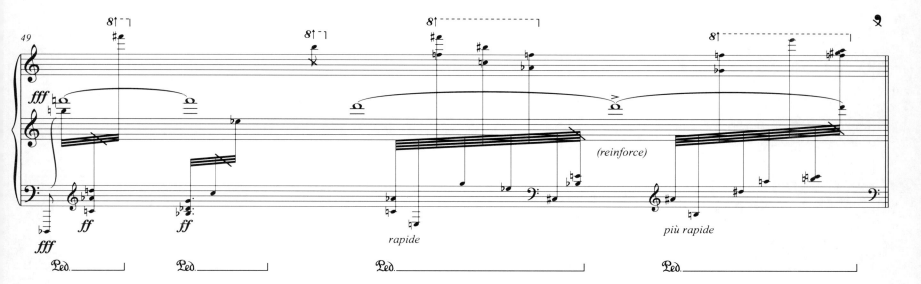

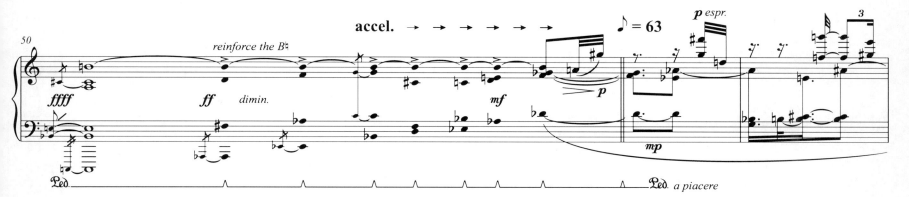

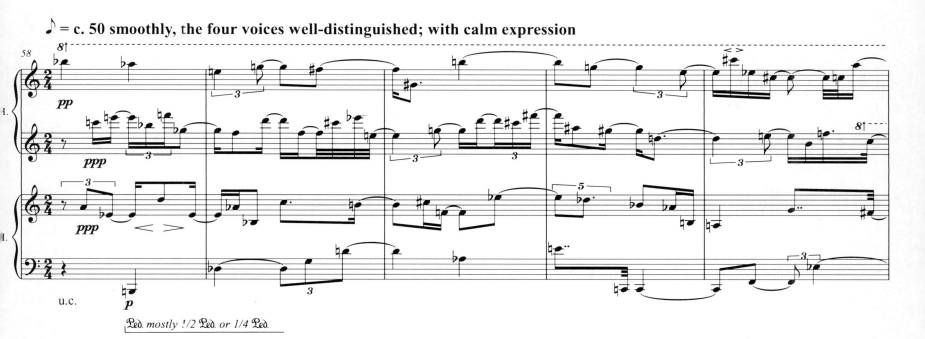

*strike and release note immediately

46

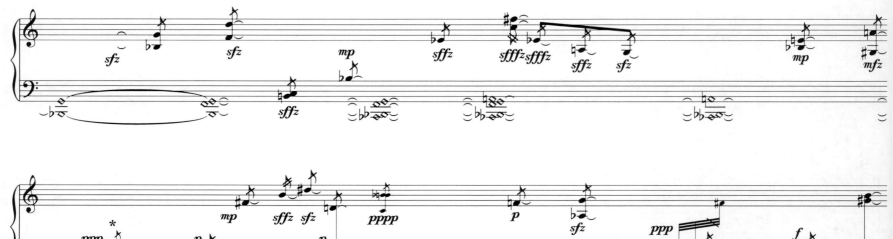

September 21, 1965

Berlin - Florence - Seattle

*the small grace-notes played so softly as not to ring.